A Model Code of Ethics for North Carolina Local Elected Officials

With Guidelines and Appendixes

A. Fleming Bell, II

UNC
SCHOOL OF
GOVERNMENT

About the Series

Local Government Board Builders offers local elected leaders practical advice on how to effectively lead and govern. Each of the booklets in this series provides a topic overview, specific tips on effective practice, and worksheets and reflection questions to help local elected leaders improve their work. The series focuses on common activities for local governing boards, such as selecting and appointing committees and advisory boards, planning for the future, making better decisions, improving board accountability, and effectively engaging stakeholders in public decisions.

Vaughn Mamlin Upshaw, lecturer in public administration and government at the UNC School of Government, is the series editor.

The School of Government at the University of North Carolina at Chapel Hill works to improve the lives of North Carolinians by engaging in practical scholarship that helps public officials and citizens understand and improve state and local government. Established in 1931 as the Institute of Government, the School provides educational, advisory, and research services for state and local governments. The School of Government is also home to a nationally ranked graduate program in public administration and specialized centers focused on information technology, environmental finance, and civic education for youth.

As the largest university-based local government training, advisory, and research organization in the United States, the School of Government offers up to 200 courses, seminars, and specialized conferences for more than 12,000 public officials each year. In addition, faculty members annually publish approximately fifty books, book chapters, bulletins, and other reference works related to state and local government. Each day that the General Assembly is in session, the School produces the *Daily Bulletin*, which reports on the day's activities for members of the legislature and others who need to follow the course of legislation.

The Master of Public Administration Program is a full-time, two-year program that serves up to sixty students annually. It consistently ranks among the best public administration graduate programs in the country, particularly in city management. With courses ranging from public policy analysis to ethics and management, the program educates leaders for local, state, and federal governments and nonprofit organizations.

Operating support for the School of Government's programs and activities comes from many sources, including state appropriations, local government membership dues, private contributions, publication sales, course fees, and service contracts. Visit www.sog.unc.edu or call 919.966.5381 for more information on the School's courses, publications, programs, and services.

Michael R. Smith, Dean
Thomas H. Thornburg, Senior Associate Dean
Frayda S. Bluestein, Associate Dean for Faculty Development
Todd A. Nicolet, Associate Dean for Operations
Ann Cary Simpson, Associate Dean for Development and Communications
Bradley G. Volk, Associate Dean for Administration

Faculty

Gregory S. Allison	Alyson A. Grine	Christopher B. McLaughlin	Carl W. Stenberg III
David N. Ammons	Norma Houston (on leave)	Kara A. Millonzi	John B. Stephens
Ann M. Anderson	Cheryl Daniels Howell	Jill D. Moore	Charles A. Szypszak
A. Fleming Bell, II	Jeffrey A. Hughes	Jonathan Q. Morgan	Shannon H. Tufts
Maureen M. Berner	Willow S. Jacobson	Ricardo S. Morse	Vaughn Mamlin Upshaw
Mark F. Botts	Robert P. Joyce	C. Tyler Mulligan	A. John Vogt
Joan G. Brannon	Kenneth L. Joyner	David W. Owens	Aimee N. Wall
Michael Crowell	Diane M. Juffras	William C. Rivenbark	Jeffrey B. Welty
Shea Riggsbee Denning	David M. Lawrence	Dale J. Roenigk	Richard B. Whisnant
James C. Drennan	Dona G. Lewandowski	John Rubin	Gordon P. Whitaker
Richard D. Ducker	James M. Markham	John L. Saxon	Eileen R. Youens
Robert L. Farb	Janet Mason	Jessica Smith	
Joseph S. Ferrell	Laurie L. Mesibov	Karl W. Smith	

Printed in the United States of America
21 20 19 18 17   2 3 4 5 6
ISBN 978-1-56011-650-9

Contents

Acknowledgments

While this guidebook is a publication of the UNC School of Government, its development has truly been a group project. A code drafting advisory committee comprising North Carolina local government officials and representatives from the North Carolina Association of County Commissioners and the North Carolina League of Municipalities played the most important role in this development.

Beginning in the fall of 2009, the committee reviewed, discussed, and revised several drafts of the Model Code of Ethics and other parts of this guidebook that I presented to them, with thoroughness, cheerfulness, and no compensation for their efforts other than the School's and my gratitude. The committee members are:

> Regina W. Alexander, city clerk, City of Southport
> Alan Andrews, assistant city attorney, City of Winston-Salem
> James B. Blackburn III, legislative counsel, North Carolina Association of
>   County Commissioners
> Wendell M. Davis, deputy county manager, Durham County
> Kimberly Smith Hibbard, general counsel, North Carolina League of
>   Municipalities
> The Honorable Susan W. Kluttz, mayor, City of Salisbury
> Patrice Roesler, deputy director, North Carolina Association of
>   County Commissioners
> Kathy Young, clerk to the Mitchell County Board of Commissioners
> The Honorable Steve Yuhasz, commissioner, Orange County

I am deeply in their debt for their extraordinary contributions in seeing this project through to a successful completion. I also give special thanks to JoAnn Brewer, School of Government program manager, who provided excellent staff support for the committee.

Many other persons also reviewed the manuscript and provided very useful comments and suggestions. In particular, I thank Debra Bechtel, Catawba County attorney; Jimmie B. Hicks, Jr., Craven County attorney; David A. Holec, Greenville city attorney;

Ralph D. Karpinos, Chapel Hill town attorney; Mark Payne, Guilford County attorney; Steve B. Settlemyer, Morganton city attorney; and Lowell Siler, Durham County attorney. I am also grateful to Charles Archer, associate director for operations and federal relations, North Carolina League of Municipalities and to my School of Government colleagues Frayda S. Bluestein, Norma Houston, Vaughn Mamlin Upshaw, and Eileen Youens for their time, expertise, and encouragement. They all helped to make this guidebook a better publication.

Finally, I thank Mike Smith, dean of the School of Government, and Tom Thornburg, senior associate dean, for entrusting me with this assignment and for providing the resources and support necessary to complete it.

Because of the nature of this type of project, I have not been able to include in the final publication every suggestion and idea proposed. However, I have tried to consider all of them carefully. In particular, I have sought to honor the committee's primary goal—to produce a legally sound, understandable, and practical guidebook for North Carolina local elected officials. Any shortcomings and mistakes in the final product are of course my responsibility.

I hope the officials for whom the guidebook is intended will consider its ideas carefully and that they will find it a useful resource as they prepare their own codes of ethics.

A. Fleming Bell, II
Professor of Public Law and Government
UNC School of Government
March 2010

Introduction

A New Statutory Requirement

The 2009 North Carolina General Assembly passed a law requiring all North Carolina cities, counties, local boards of education, unified governments, sanitary districts, and consolidated city-counties to adopt a resolution or policy containing a code of ethics to guide actions by the governing board members in the performance of their official duties as members of that governing board.[1] Each governing board must adopt its resolution or policy by January 1, 2011.

This guidebook is intended to help local elected boards and their staff members develop codes of ethics that meet the statutory requirements. It includes a Model Code with optional provisions as well as commentary and discussion questions that boards are encouraged to use in developing and interpreting their own codes of ethics.

This Guidebook's Approach

The Model Code sets out a comprehensive statement of guiding ethical principles, based on the specific requirements of G.S. 160A-86.[2] Local government officials will find it useful to return regularly to these principles as they develop and interpret their own code provisions.

The statement of principles is based on the assumption that the public trust can only be preserved if elected officials are serious about their calling and make informed decisions that reflect core ethical principles they hold in common with the citizens they represent.

---

1. N.C. Gen. Stat. (hereinafter G.S.) § 160A-86. This statute was originally enacted as G.S. 160A-83 by Session Law (S.L.) 2009-403. It was codified by the revisor of statutes as G.S. 160A-86. The law, which took effect January 1, 2010, also requires that all elected local governing board members receive two clock hours of ethics training by January 1, 2011, and again within twelve months of each reappointment or reelection thereafter. See G.S. 160A-87 (G.S. 160A-84 prior to codification). The text of S.L. 2009-403 may be found in Appendix 3.

2. G.S. 160A-86 was originally adopted as G.S. 160A-83. See Note 1 for the explanation of renumbering.

Making such decisions requires the development of skills in ethical policy-making rather than simply the memorization of rules. It also requires understanding the difference between the spirit and the letter of the law. Elected officials must serve as "especially responsible citizens"[3] who model ethical behavior in their communities.

The ethical principles outlined in the guidebook are supplemented by a commentary that applies these principles to some specific situations that are likely to occur. Alternative wordings are also provided for many provisions, in recognition that boards will wish to take a variety of approaches in their codes.

The guidebook reflects the fact that one must be realistic about what can and cannot legally be required in codes adopted pursuant to G.S. 160A-86. Some patterns of behavior that might be desirable in board members might only be achieved by the good faith efforts of the individual board members themselves rather than by a code of ethics.

For example, it may be a good idea for board members to inform the public and each other about any financial affairs that may pose conflicts with their public duties. A local governing board, however, simply does not have the power to require its members to provide financial disclosure statements.[4]

In addition, local elected governing boards do not have legal authority to forbid a member from engaging in conduct that reflects poorly on the community. They must rely on persuasion rather than law to encourage the member to behave differently. They should also be willing to listen to the member's point of view rather than lashing out in a manner that is disrespectful or that may not be based on all of the facts.

The remedies a local board may employ when its code is violated are quite limited under current North Carolina law. The principal response available to a board when one of its members violates its code is to expose the issue and to express its displeasure by adopting a resolution of censure. This resolution can be discussed and approved publicly and incorporated in the board's minutes as a permanent record that expresses the sentiments of the majority of the board. Such a resolution has no legal effect, however. It is in no way binding on the member who is censured. If the board or any of its members believes that a board member has violated a state criminal statute, the matter may be referred to the local district attorney for possible prosecution. Appendix 1 explains some of the specific

---

3. Terry L. Cooper, *The Responsible Administrator: An Approach to Ethics for the Administrative Role*, 4th ed. (San Francisco: Jossey-Bass, 1998), 48 (quoting Paul Appleby).

4. The only exception would be if the General Assembly passed a local act granting this power to a particular local government. See also the introductory text to "Optional Section on Censure of Board Members."

behaviors that local board members should practice in order to avoid violating state statutes dealing with conflicts of interest.[5]

Scope of Local Codes

Under G.S. 160A-86 all North Carolina cities, counties, local boards of education, unified governments, sanitary districts, and consolidated city-counties must, by January 1, 2011, adopt a resolution or policy containing a code of ethics to guide actions by the governing board members in the performance of their official duties as board members. The code must address at least five key board member responsibilities.[6] These responsibilities reflect concern for ethical principles as well as for the effects of the board members' decisions on others.

The five areas to be addressed are as follows (emphases and comments added):

1. The need *to obey all applicable laws* regarding official actions taken as a board member.
   Comment: For example, the member must honor the oath of office, in which the member swore to uphold the constitution and laws.[7]
2. The need *to uphold the integrity and independence* of the board member's office.
   Comment: Among other things, this principle requires board members to make decisions based on the public good and not on their desires or considerations of special interests.
3. The need *to avoid impropriety* in the exercise of the board member's official duties.
   Comment: Board members are to act as "especially responsible citizens" who are to honor the public trust as they carry out their duties. Their official actions should be above reproach.

---

5. Federal law imposes further ethical requirements on local governments that receive grants from the federal government. Those requirements are beyond the scope of this guidebook, which is focused on the provisions of G.S. 160A-86. Local officials with federal grants should consult their attorneys as well as reviewing two posts by Eileen Youens of the UNC School of Government published in the School's online blog, *Coates' Canons*. See Eileen Youens, "Protests and ARRA and Bears, Oh My!," *Coates' Canons*, UNC School of Government, October 27, 2009, http://sogweb.sog.unc.edu/blogs/localgovt/?p=1129, and "Federal Grants and Contracts Management," *Coates' Canons*, UNC School of Government, November 4, 2009, http://sogweb.sog.unc.edu/blogs/localgovt/?p=1185&cpage=1#comment-180. See also the sources cited in those posts, as well as the follow-up questions and Youens's responses.

6. G.S. 160A-86.

7. N.C. Const. art. VI, § 7. The text of the oath is set out in Appendix 3.

4. The need *to faithfully perform* the duties of the office.

   Comment: A public official who acts faithfully is one whom others can trust and respect.

5. The need *to conduct the affairs of the governing board in an open and public manner*, including complying with all applicable laws concerning open meetings and public records.

   Comment: A public official who is honest, fair, kind, and compassionate and who conscientiously upholds the public trust will honor the spirit as well as the letter of the law. He or she will see openness or transparency as an important part of that responsibility.

The statute leaves local boards a good deal of leeway in deciding what their codes will contain, as long as the code addresses the five topics listed above. The code may be very detailed, or it may be very general. It may describe behavior the board's members and the board as a whole should strive toward or behavior board members should avoid.

Enforcement of Local Codes

As noted earlier, G.S. 160A-86 does not describe or authorize sanctions or other means of enforcing locally adopted ethics codes. Legal action can only be taken if a board member's behavior violates some other law, such as the state's criminal law, the open meetings or public records law, or a common law or constitutional limitation that affects governmental actions.[8]

When a board member does not comply with the code, the rest of the board can do little other than adopting a resolution censuring the member. It is hoped board members will choose to avoid impropriety and obey all applicable laws, but they cannot be forced to do so by the board. The board must rely on voluntary adherence to the code and to other laws.

8. See, e.g., G.S. 14-230 (neglect of duty); G.S. 14-234 (conflicts of interest in contracting); G.S. 14-234.1 (misuse of confidential information); G.S. 143-318.16 to -318.16C (remedy provisions under the open meetings statutes); G.S. 132-9 (remedy provisions under the public records statutes); and 133-32 (gifts and favors). All of these statutes are reprinted in Appendix 3, and some are discussed in Appendix 1. As suggested in the text, constitutional rules such as those governing procedural due process are also relevant, as is the common law governing conflicts of interest generally. Board members may obtain more information about procedural due process and common law conflicts by contacting the board's attorney and the UNC School of Government.

This is not to suggest, however, that codes of ethics should restate existing law that is separately enforceable by the district attorney or other persons. Including such restatements in a local code is redundant and may be confusing to board members and citizens.

An optional section describing procedures for censure is included at the end of the code. In addition, Appendix 1 provides guidelines for behavior that may help board members avoid violation of existing laws relating to conflicts of interest and voting.

A Model Code of Ethics

The Text of the Model Code

Boards are specifically authorized to look to model local government codes of ethics for guidance in developing resolutions or policies that include a code of ethics. The Model Code that follows is designed to assist local governments with this task. The Comments provide guidance to local elected officials in understanding the Code's contents and purpose and are not intended to be part of the Code.

The Model Code of Ethics is divided into several parts: a "Preamble," a "Statement of General Principles," and the "Code of Ethics" itself. The Code includes a statement of purpose, five sections that correspond to the five subject areas addressed by G.S. 160A-86, and an optional section on censure procedures.

Local officials should probably examine and discuss this guidebook at length before beginning to draft a code of ethics for their jurisdiction. Each local governing board will confront a number of questions as it decides on the type of code that will best suit the board. The Model Code, commentary, and other materials are intended to help local officials address those questions in a practical, straightforward manner.[1]

The Comment portion for each section of the Code includes several questions designed to promote discussion. It is hoped local boards will find these aids useful.[2]

Local boards and the public will both benefit greatly from engaging in a thorough discussion and debate before a code of ethics is adopted. This means, for example, that adoption of a local code of ethics should certainly *not* be a consent agenda item, if a board is acting responsibly and thoughtfully. Indeed, the Model Code will not have served its purpose if it does not stimulate such thoughtful consideration.

---

1. Other useful examples of codes of ethics may be found in A. Fleming Bell, II, *Ethics, Conflicts, and Offices: A Guide for Local Officials*, 2d ed. (Chapel Hill: UNC School of Government, forthcoming spring 2010).
2. Thanks to Vaughn M. Upshaw of the UNC School of Government for authoring most of the questions.

After adopting their codes, boards should also periodically reexamine them to ensure they remain up to date. A community's needs and the conditions it confronts will frequently change over time.

The Commentary and the Optional Provisions of the Model Code

Each section of the Model Code is followed by commentary describing in more detail the principles involved and giving examples where appropriate. As noted above, the commentary is not officially part of the Code but is intended to provide information and guidance to local elected officials in their consideration of the Code's provisions.

Each Code section states that local elected officials "should," rather than "shall," obey the provisions of that particular section. This choice of language reflects the legal limitations on a local board's authority to sanction a member who chooses not to follow a local code provision. As noted earlier, adoption of a nonbinding resolution of censure is generally the only action a board may take against one of its members. See the optional section on censure procedures at the end of the Model Code.

The Model Code takes an approach that is somewhat of a hybrid between "aspirational" and "prohibitive" codes, as those terms are described in Appendix 2. It sets out core ethical principles toward which elected officials aspire while at the same time stating what those officials should in fact do.

In some instances optional additions to the Code are also provided. These additions are intended to provide some guidance for boards that may wish to say a bit more than is included in the "standard" language of the Code. Local boards may adopt as many or as few of these provisions as they wish.

In a few cases, alternative wordings are provided. The board is again free to choose whichever version it prefers.

The board may also draft other standard or optional language as it chooses. However, two cautions are in order. First, the language must meet the requirements of G.S. 160A-86 (see "Scope of Local Codes," above). Second, the board must *not* include code provisions that might violate other laws. For example, as noted earlier, in most cases adoption of a nonbinding resolution of censure is the only remedy available under North Carolina law to a board in the event of a board member's perceived misbehavior. The board does *not* have the power to provide for other punishments, except in the very rare case it is specifically authorized to do so by a local act of the General Assembly.[3]

3. See also the introductory text to "Optional Section on Censure of Board Members."

The Model Code

Code of Ethics for the
___[Board's Official Name]___ of
[Name of City, County, Sanitary District, School Administrative Unit, Unified Government, or Consolidated City-County], North Carolina

PREAMBLE

WHEREAS, the Constitution of North Carolina, Article I, Section 35, reminds us that a "frequent recurrence to fundamental principles is absolutely necessary to preserve the blessings of liberty," and

WHEREAS, a spirit of honesty and forthrightness is reflected in North Carolina's state motto, *Esse quam videri*, "To be rather than to seem," and

WHEREAS, Section 160A-86 of the North Carolina General Statutes requires local governing boards to adopt a code of ethics, and

WHEREAS, as public officials we are charged with upholding the trust of the citizens of this [jurisdiction], and with obeying the law, and

WHEREAS, __[other clauses that jurisdiction may desire]__

NOW THEREFORE, in recognition of our blessings and obligations as citizens of the State of North Carolina and as public officials representing the citizens of the __[type of jurisdiction]__ of __[name of jurisdiction]__, and acting pursuant to the requirements of Section 160A-86 of the North Carolina General Statutes, we the [official name of governing board] do hereby adopt the following General Principles and Code of Ethics to guide the [type of governing board] in its lawful decision-making.

GENERAL PRINCIPLES UNDERLYING THE CODE OF ETHICS

- The stability and proper operation of democratic representative government depend upon public confidence in the integrity of the government and upon responsible exercise of the trust conferred by the people upon their elected officials.
- Governmental decisions and policy must be made and implemented through proper channels and processes of the governmental structure.
- Board members must be able to act in a manner that maintains their integrity and independence, yet is responsive to the interests and needs of those they represent.

- Board members must always remain aware that at various times they play different roles:
  - As advocates, who strive to advance the legitimate needs of their citizens
  - As legislators, who balance the public interest and private rights in considering and enacting ordinances, orders, and resolutions
  - As decision-makers, who arrive at fair and impartial quasi-judicial and administrative determinations.
- Board members must know how to distinguish among these roles, to determine when each role is appropriate, and to act accordingly.
- Board members must be aware of their obligation to conform their behavior to standards of ethical conduct that warrant the trust of their constituents. Each official must find within his or her own conscience the touchstone by which to determine what conduct is appropriate.

CODE OF ETHICS

The purpose of this Code of Ethics is to establish guidelines for ethical standards of conduct for the [official name of governing board] and to help determine what conduct is appropriate in particular cases. It should not be considered a substitute for the law or for a board member's best judgment.

Questions for Discussion

Why is it important (other than being required by law) for your board to have a code of ethics?

_____

_____

_____

_____

How complete do you find the "General Principles Underlying the Code of Ethics"? What additional statements does your board want to add to the "Whereas" clauses at the beginning of the Code? Are there any parts of the beginning section that the board wishes to remove?

_____
_____
_____
_____

How might ethical conduct vary when the board is functioning in an advocacy, legislative, or quasi-judicial role?

_____
_____
_____
_____

What actions do you and others on your board take to preserve the public's trust?

_____
_____
_____
_____

How do you balance your individual interests with your representative role? How do you decide whether to vote your conscience or to follow apparent public opinion as it may be expressed in citizen communications at a hearing, through letters or e-mail, or at the polls?

_____
_____
_____
_____

> Section 1. Board members should obey all laws applicable to their official actions as members of the board. Board members should be guided by the spirit as well as the letter of the law in whatever they do.
>
> At the same time, board members should feel free to assert policy positions and opinions without fear of reprisal from fellow board members or citizens. To declare that a board member is behaving unethically because one disagrees with that board member on a question of policy (and not because of the board member's behavior) is unfair, dishonest, irresponsible, and itself unethical.

Comment. While it is of course unrealistic to expect an official to know every law, rule, and regulation that exists at a given time, officials should take seriously the pledge to protect and support the state and federal constitutions and laws that they swore or affirmed as part of the oath of office.[4]

This pledge may mean different things in different contexts. For example, if a local official is ever in doubt about what course of conduct is legal in a particular situation, the official should seek the advice of the local government's attorney. If the official is in doubt about what course of action is ethical, as opposed to legal, the official should seek the counsel of other board members and trusted advisors, again including the government's attorney. Appendix 1 contains a helpful list and discussion of behaviors that are required in order to comply with North Carolina's various conflict of interest laws for local governments.

While acting ethically can also generally ensure that one is acting legally, this is not always the case. For example, the voting statutes for city councils and county commissioners specifically require these officials to vote in all cases where their "own financial interest or official conduct" is not involved, even though the official may think a situation involves an ethical conflict.[5] This means, for instance, that a board member might be required to make a decision affecting a relative, even though the official has a personal non-financial interest in the outcome of the decision. The

---

4. The constitutional oath of office may be found in Article VI, Section 7, of the North Carolina Constitution. It is reprinted in Appendix 3.

5. See G.S. 153A-44 and G.S. 160A-75. The text of both statutes is included in Appendix 3, and they are among the laws addressed in Appendix 1. See also A. Fleming Bell, II, *Ethics, Conflicts, and Offices: A Guide for Local Officials*, 2d ed., Chapters 4 and 5 (Chapel Hill: UNC School of Government, forthcoming spring 2010).

ethical conflict does not absolve the official from his or her voting responsibility under the law, no matter how uncomfortable voting makes the official feel.

It is sometimes suggested that a possible way around this situation is to ask to be excused from the meeting, as opposed to being excused from voting, or simply not to appear at the meeting until the board has dealt with the item in question. While this action may be legal, it may not be the most ethically responsible solution. Public officials are expected to attend meetings and to vote.

Statutes governing land use development decisions modify this rule.[6] The provisions that must be followed in land use cases are spelled out in G.S. 153A-340(g), and G.S. 160A-381(d), which establish statutory standards for conflicts of interest in legislative planning and zoning decision-making for county and city governing boards and other boards performing such functions; and in G.S. 153A-345(e1) and G.S. 160A-388(e1), which establish statutory standards for boards performing quasi-judicial functions in the land use area. In the latter case, the governing or other board may be able to vote to prevent a member who is prohibited from participating in a decision by the land use quasi-judicial conflict of interest statutes from tainting the board's action by that member's involvement.

The board must always be mindful of other relevant statutes that govern its decisions, regardless of its code. As we have just seen, specific statutes control voting by city and county governing board members on land use matters, regardless of what language may be included in the local governing board's code of ethics. Other specific laws establishing standards of conduct that board members must obey include G.S. 14-230 (willful failure to discharge duties); G.S. 14-234 (benefiting from public contracts by public officers or employees); G.S. 14-234.1 (misuse of confidential information); G.S. Chapter 143, Article 33C (meetings of public bodies); G.S. Chapter 132 (public records); and G.S. 133-32 (regulation of gifts and favors). The text of many of these statutes is included in Appendix 3, and some of them are discussed in Appendix 1.[7] As noted in Section 3 of the Model Code and elsewhere in this guidebook, while board members must obey the statutes, the board has no power to enforce the law against its members.

The Model Code strongly cautions elected officials that they should obey the spirit as well as the letter of the law in whatever they do. "Splitting hairs" will generally not be well-received by citizens, the press, and one's fellow board members, who may regard questionable behavior as unseemly even if not illegal. However, it must be recognized

---

6. See G.S. 153A-340(g) and G.S. 160A-381(d) (legislative decisions) and G.S. 153A-345(e1) and G.S. 160A-388(e1) (quasi-judicial decisions). These statutes are included in Appendix 3 and are discussed in Appendix 1.

7. See also the Comment to Section 3b of the Model Code.

that public office is inherently part of a political process within which different people and groups have varying opinions and seek different results. Politicians sometimes couch policy arguments in assertions that their opponents are behaving unethically. This section makes clear that such assertions are themselves dishonest, unfair, and irresponsible and hence unethical. Honest policy disagreements are part of our democratic system and are to be encouraged, not quashed.

Optional Addition to Section 1.
[Board members should endeavor to keep up to date, through the board's attorney and other sources, about new or ongoing legal or ethical issues they may face in their official positions. This educational function is in addition to the day-to-day legal advice the board may receive concerning specific situations that arise.]

[**Comment.** This optional section recognizes that many local attorneys, as well as organizations such as the UNC School of Government, the N.C. Association of County Commissioners, and the N.C. League of Municipalities, often serve as important educational resources for board members, as well as being trusted advisors on particular legal matters.]

Optional Addition to Section 1.
[Board members should endeavor to keep up to date, through the board's attorney and other sources, about the most pertinent constitutional, statutory, and other legal requirements with which they must be familiar to meet their legal responsibilities. The board should consider adopting a list of applicable laws and regulations, with appropriate commentary, as a reference document accompanying this Code.]

[**Comment.** In order to keep the Model Code of Ethics brief and to the point, and to avoid overlooking some of the many important statutes on a variety of topics related to ethics and other subjects that guide local officials, the text of pertinent laws is, for the most part, not included in this Model Code. At the same time, some local boards will probably like to have ready reference materials for those laws that they are sworn to uphold with which they are most regularly involved.

To meet this need, this optional section allows the board to direct its attorney or other advisor to prepare and maintain for its use both a list of these statutes and a commentary about them. Technically speaking, this list would generally not be an official part of the local code. However, the board may adopt it as a reference work or appendix to accompany the main code document.

Another very useful source for the most pertinent laws affecting North Carolina local governments is *Administrative and Financial Laws for Local Government in North Carolina*, available from the UNC School of Government. This publication includes the contracting conflicts of interest and gifts and favors statutes (G.S. 14-234, G.S 14-234.1, and G.S. 133-32), as well as laws dealing with how city and county governing boards take action, multiple office-holding, financial and budgeting requirements for local governments, and oaths of office, among other topics.

Elected officials and their attorneys may also find very useful a summary of advice and cautions concerning some common legal situations they may encounter in the areas of contracting and, for city and county board members, voting. It was prepared by Frayda S. Bluestein of the UNC School of Government and is reproduced in Appendix 1.

As it learns more about the law, the board should continue to keep in mind the admonition above. While board members must of course obey the statutes, the board has no power to enforce the law against its members. That role belongs to others such as the local district attorney.[8]]

Questions for Discussion
What does it mean to you to obey the law? Do you feel differently about this idea now than before you took office?

_____
_____
_____
_____

---

8. See also the Comment to Section 3b of the Model Code.

What do you think of the idea that local governing boards cannot enforce the law against their members? Should they be able to do so? Would more robust enforcement tools be helpful, or would they lead to abuse?

_____

_____

_____

_____

How might your board successfully encourage ethical behavior among its members?

_____

_____

_____

How might you best keep up with all of the laws and regulations that you are to obey as a governing board member? To what extent will the suggestions in the optional additions to Section 1 help you?

_____

_____

_____

_____

<u>Section 2</u>. Board members should act with integrity and independence from improper influence as they exercise the duties of their offices. Characteristics and behaviors consistent with this standard include the following:

- Adhering firmly to a code of sound values
- Behaving consistently and with respect toward everyone with whom they interact
- Exhibiting trustworthiness
- Living as if they are on duty as elected officials regardless of where they are or what they doing
- Using their best independent judgment to pursue the common good as they see it, presenting their opinions to all in a reasonable, forthright, consistent manner
- Remaining incorruptible, self-governing, and unaffected by improper influence while at the same time being able to consider the opinions and ideas of others
- Disclosing contacts and information about issues that they receive outside of public meetings and refraining from seeking or receiving information about quasi-judicial matters outside of the quasi-judicial proceedings themselves
- Treating other board members and the public with respect and honoring the opinions of others even when the board members disagree with those opinions
- Not reaching conclusions on issues until all sides have been heard
- Showing respect for their offices and not behaving in ways that reflect badly on those offices
- Recognizing that they are part of a larger group and acting accordingly
- Recognizing that individual board members are not generally allowed to act on behalf of the board but may only do so if the board specifically authorizes it, and that the board must take official action as a body

Comment. The dictionary defines *integrity*[9] as "firm adherence to a code of especially moral or artistic values." It can also mean soundness or completeness. We have all known people who especially embody this quality—they know who they are and they act in accordance with the same high standards, no matter what they are doing

9. *Merriam-Webster's Collegiate Dictionary*, 11th ed., s.v. "integrity."

or who is or is not watching. They are faithful, trustworthy, respectful of others, and incorruptible.

Officials who act with integrity generally assume that they are on duty at all times—that the oath of office does not cease to operate when they engage in private activities. Indeed, they recognize that they may come under greater scrutiny then than at other times.

Persons who have independence of thought are generally self-governing individuals who are not subject to improper influence by others. While such people often look to others for opinions or guidance in conduct, they are not dependent on others' points of view or advice when making decisions.

In the public arena, independence of thought and from improper influence go hand-in-hand with integrity. An independent public official does not act in a vacuum. While public officials must act autonomously to make their own decisions based on their best judgment about what is in the public interest, they must also demonstrate firm principles and sound values.

Consistently acting with both independence and integrity is often one of the hardest tasks a public official will confront. A wide variety of persons and groups constantly clamor for elected officials' attention and support, as befits our expectations of a representative democracy. However, those persons are understandably often more concerned about their own particular position or interest than about the greater good of the community. An independent public official must be able to resist improper influence and say "no" when necessary, and an official with integrity must not equate private desires with public needs. Public officials who demonstrate independence and integrity should be able to resolve faithfully the ancient dilemma of whether they are in office to represent constituents or to act as independent leaders.

Persons of integrity realize the limitations as well as the benefits of independence. Recognizing that they are part of a larger elected group, they value the office and try not to bring it into disrepute. Respect for the other board members and for everyone else whom they encounter is essential, as is a willingness to listen to the opinions of others even if a board member disagrees with them.

Questions for Discussion

How difficult is it to act with integrity as a member of your board? As a citizen of your community?

_____
_____
_____
_____

Can you think of an example of a public official who acted improperly? Without naming names, describe the improper behavior. What, if anything, did you do or wish you had done?

_____
_____
_____
_____

How do members of your board reconcile the statutory requirement to vote on issues with the idea that doing so may in some cases appear unethical?

_____
_____
_____
_____

What, if any, ethical guidelines should elected officials follow when advocating their individual positions in public settings (for example, community events, Web blogs)?

_____
_____
_____
_____

> Section 3.a. Board members should avoid impropriety in the exercise of their official duties. Their official actions should be above reproach. Although opinions may vary about what behavior is inappropriate, this board will consider impropriety in terms of whether a reasonable person who is aware of all of the relevant facts and circumstances surrounding the board member's action would conclude that the action was inappropriate.

Comment. Consideration of propriety is important in the world of ethics. While most of us would agree that an official should be above reproach in carrying out his or her official duties, simply stating this principle does not establish a clear standard for behavior in many cases. Context often matters, and opinions may vary about what is appropriate. Even behavior that is quite innocent may appear improper in the eyes of those observing it.

At the same time, objectivity is very important if public officials are to be treated fairly by their colleagues and by citizens. The language in this section provides for determination of impropriety by an objective standard. The test for impropriety is whether a reasonable person who is aware of all of the relevant facts and circumstances surrounding the board member's action would conclude that the action was inappropriate.

Some local boards may want to explicitly prevent appearances of impropriety as well as behavior that is actually improper. They may assume that doing so promotes a higher standard of conduct from board members. However, assuming that behavior is improper simply because of how it may appear, without objective consideration of all of the facts, presents a real danger. Innocent people may be hurt if those observing such people base their conclusions on incomplete knowledge.

Consider, for example, the case of Susan the county commissioner, who is having lunch with Bob, an old friend from college. Each of them orders and pays for their own meal at the counter of a local sandwich shop and they sit down to eat. Bob tells Susan that he will soon become the sales representative for all of his company's government accounts in the area, including their account with Susan's local government. Susan explains to Bob that in the future it will be very important legally and ethically for her to avoid any involvement with the account, and Bob tells her he understands.

About that time, Jeff, a representative from one of Bob's competitors, walks into the sandwich shop. Upon seeing Bob and Susan together, he immediately concludes that Bob is seeking a more favorable contract with the county and that Bob is buying Susan lunch to help persuade her to go along. Jeff storms over to Susan's and Bob's table, demands an explanation, and then rushes out before one can be given.

Jeff sees an appearance of impropriety in Bob's and Susan's lunch together. Had he been aware of all of the facts, however—that Susan and Bob are old friends, that they each paid for their own meal, and that they were in fact talking about ways to avoid such impropriety—Jeff might have had a different reaction.

This simple story illustrates the problems that can arise from relying on an "appearance of impropriety" standard rather than on a standard that prohibits actual improper behavior. Boards must be vigilant in their efforts to be open and transparent, to identify potential appearance-of-impropriety problems, and to insist (to the extent that they can) that their members be judged fairly and objectively.

> <u>Section 3.b</u>. If a board member believes that his or her actions, while legal and ethical, may be misunderstood, the member should seek the advice of the board's attorney[10] and should consider publicly disclosing the facts of the situation and the steps taken to resolve it (such as consulting with the attorney).

Comment. As we have just seen, board members may often face dilemmas because their actions are either innocently or intentionally misunderstood. Section 3.b provides a way for board members to "clear the air" and avoid misunderstandings about apparent ethical breaches.

For city and county elected board members, the need for explanation is especially apparent in questions about voting. For example, G.S. 153A-44 (counties) and G.S. 160A-75 (cities) require governing board members to vote, with very few exceptions. A board member may be excused only if the vote involves the member's own financial interest or official conduct; certain contractual matters under G.S. 14-234; or certain land use questions under G.S. Chapter 153A, Article 18, and Chapter 160A, Article 19. In all other cases the member must vote, even if the member has a personal connection to the matter in question that would normally be

10. See the second paragraph of the Comment to Section 1.

seen as involving a conflict between the member's public and private interests.[11] For example, a member may be required to vote on funding for a new recreational center even though it is clear that the member's family will make use of the facility. Strictly speaking, funding this sort of community facility does not implicate the member's own financial interest.

A similar sort of dilemma arises when a governing board member also serves on the board of a nonprofit corporation that relies on funds from the city or county. In this case, the conflict is between two public or quasi-public interests—that of the local government in spending its money wisely and that of the nonprofit entity in receiving as much money as possible. The governing board member must participate in decisions concerning money, even though the member may feel a conflict between two different fiduciary obligations.[12]

In cases such as those just mentioned, it is extremely important that the city or county governing board member explain to the public what he or she is doing and why. While publicly acknowledging the conflict may not allay all citizen concerns, explaining that one is required by law to participate in a decision may relieve some of them.[13]

Questions for Discussion

What does propriety mean to you? Why is the concept so important for citizens and others?

_____

_____

_____

_____

11. See also the Comment to Section 1.

12. For further discussion of conflict issues when nonprofit entities are involved, see Frayda S. Bluestein, "Board Members Who Serve on Nonprofit Boards—Conflict of Interest? *Coates' Canons*, UNC School of Government, September 30, 2009, http://sogweb.sog.unc.edu/blogs/localgovt/?p=823.

13. For further discussion of the legal and ethical requirements for voting that apply to city and county governing boards, please see A. Fleming Bell, II, *Ethics, Conflicts, and Offices: A Guide for Local Officials*, 2d ed., Chapter 4 (Chapel Hill: UNC School of Government, forthcoming spring 2010).

Have you ever been misjudged, as were Bob and Susan in the example in the Comment? What was the situation? What did you do?

_____
_____
_____
_____

Should a governing board member serve on the board of a nonprofit organization to which the member's governmental unit provides money? As an employee of the organization? As a volunteer fund-raiser for the organization? Give reasons for your answers.

_____
_____
_____
_____

Should local governments refrain from giving money to organizations with which their governing board members are involved? Why or why not?

_____
_____
_____
_____

To what extent do you feel obliged to explain your behavior to others when you are acting ethically and legally but there is an "appearance issue" (for example, when you are legally required to vote on a matter involving one of your relatives)?

_____
_____
_____
_____

What local situations raise questions or increase the risk of impropriety for your board (for example, social events in one another's homes, joint purchase of vacation property)?

_____
_____
_____
_____

<u>Section 4</u>. Board members should faithfully perform the duties of their offices. They should act as the especially responsible citizens[14] whom others can trust and respect. They should set a good example for others in the community, keeping in mind that trust and respect must continually be earned.

Board members should faithfully attend and prepare for meetings. They should carefully analyze all credible information properly submitted to them, mindful of the need not to engage in communications outside the meeting in quasi-judicial matters. They should demand full accountability from those over whom the board has authority.

Board members should be willing to bear their fair share of the board's workload. To the extent appropriate, they should be willing to put the board's interests ahead of their own.

Comment. Faithfulness is another word commonly heard in ethics circles but often not fully defined. This Model Code uses three related terms—responsibility, trust, and respect—to attempt to explain what it means. Someone who is faithful in the performance of his or her duties is likely to be someone whom others trust and respect. In the public arena, such persons are sometimes referred to as "especially responsible citizens"[15]—that is, they are trusted to act as representatives on behalf of all of us.

To be faithful as an elected board member, one must attend required meetings and come prepared to engage in the business of the board or committee. Board members must also demand accountability from others in order to help preserve the trust and respect of their citizens. In many cases, not all persons and entities working for or doing business with the local government will report directly to the governing board. However, the board must insist on being adequately informed so it can effectively and responsibly govern.

Members should also foster trust among themselves by acting responsibly and by putting the board's interests ahead of their own to the extent appropriate. Thus, for example, a faithful board member should bear his or her fair share of the elected board's workload. As another example, a board member should generally be willing

14. Terry L. Cooper, *The Responsible Administrator: An Approach to Ethics for the Administrative Role*, 4th ed. (San Francisco: Jossey-Bass, 1998), 48 (quoting Paul Appleby).

15. Ibid.

to keep confidential information from legally called and held closed sessions and to keep private information that the board's attorney has determined is confidential.

Board members' loyalty to the group should not be absolute, however. In some instances, the interests of the majority of the board may be at odds with those of the community the board members were elected to serve. If a board member conscientiously decides that he or she must refuse to go along with actions being taken by the rest of the board, the member should take whatever responsible steps are necessary to keep faith with the citizens and explain openly and respectfully his or her decision.

Questions for Discussion

What does it mean to faithfully perform one's duties as a board member? Can you give specific examples?

_____
_____
_____
_____

What does it mean to bear one's fair share of the workload as a board member?

_____
_____
_____
_____

To what extent should a board member put the board's interests ahead of his or her own?

_____
_____
_____
_____

How does a member determine whether his or her conscience requires the member to "go his or her own way"?

_____
_____
_____
_____

How do members of the board maintain a culture of civility? That is to say, are people on your board able to disagree without being disagreeable?

_____
_____
_____
_____

Section 5. Board members should conduct the affairs of the board in an open and public manner. They should comply with all applicable laws governing open meetings and public records, recognizing that doing so is an important way to be worthy of the public's trust. They should remember when they meet that they are conducting the public's business. They should also remember that local government records belong to the public and not to board members or their employees.

In order to ensure strict compliance with the laws concerning openness, board members should make clear that an environment of transparency and candor is to be maintained at all times in the governmental unit. They should prohibit unjustified delay in fulfilling public records requests. They should take deliberate steps to make certain that any closed sessions held by the board are lawfully conducted and that such sessions do not stray from the purposes for which they are called.

Comment. If citizens are to have faith in their local governments and trust their local officials to make decisions in the public's best interest, they must have information about what those governments and officials are planning and doing. The law of North Carolina acknowledges this fact in some of the first paragraphs of the state's open meetings and public records statutes, included below. These provisions recognize the citizens as the ultimate beneficiaries of the open meetings and public records laws.

The preamble of the open meetings law states:

> Whereas the public bodies that administer the legislative, policy-making, quasi-judicial, administrative, and advisory functions of North Carolina and its political subdivisions exist solely to conduct the people's business, it is the public policy of North Carolina that the hearings, deliberations, and actions of these bodies be conducted openly.[16]

Similarly, the General Assembly has provided for very broad access to public records in North Carolina, unless a specific statute exempts a particular record from disclosure. According to the public records law,

> The public records and public information compiled by the agencies of North Carolina government or its subdivisions are the property of the

16. G.S. 143-318.9.

people. Therefore, it is the policy of this State that the people may obtain copies of their public records and public information free or at minimal cost unless otherwise specifically provided by law. As used herein, "minimal cost" shall mean the actual cost of reproducing the public record or public information.[17]

The importance of transparency to the General Assembly is underscored by the fact that complying with open meetings and public records law is mentioned twice in the statutory guidelines for local codes of ethics. The fifth requirement specifically calls for compliance "with all applicable laws governing open meetings and public records." At the same time, the first requirement stresses the need "to obey all applicable laws regarding official actions taken as a board member," which would include actions relating to meetings and to records.

Hence, Section 5 emphasizes openness. This emphasis is in keeping with the open meetings and public records laws as well as with the statutory requirements for local codes of ethics. Local boards must also be mindful, however, of extraordinary situations recognized in the statutes as calling for closed sessions or confidential records.

Violations of the open meetings and public records laws can have real legal and financial consequences and can also cause bad publicity and a loss of citizen trust in government. See G.S. 143-318.16 to G.S. 143-318.17, set out in Appendix 3, for a description of the potential effects of violating the open meetings statute, and G.S. 132-9, also in Appendix 3, for a similar outline in the public records law.

To elected officials and their staff members, it may sometimes seem easier to govern if citizens would simply leave them alone, not asking questions and not seeking information. However, an ethical democratic society is based on openness, trust, and honesty, all of which are values that laws relating to greater transparency promote. The requirements of G.S. 160A-86 and of the open meetings and public records laws are intended to foster such a society.

To some extent, Section 5 may be considered the linchpin that holds the entire Model Code together. It would be difficult for a citizen to judge whether an elected governing board is following the tenets in Sections 1 through 4 unless the board adheres to the principles of Section 5.

---

17. G.S. 132-1(b). In addition to charging the direct cost of duplicating the record, a reasonable special service charge may be assessed if the request requires extensive use of information technology resources or extensive clerical or supervisory assistance, and in other limited cases. G.S. 132-6.2(b)

Section 5 implicitly assumes that citizens and others who ask for information about their local government will do so in an open and respectful manner. To the extent this is not the case, local elected and appointed officials should nevertheless scrupulously obey the letter and the spirit of the law and the code of ethics when dealing with any person they are privileged to serve.

Questions for Discussion

What does transparency in government mean to you? Is it limited to opening meetings and sharing records, or does it involve other areas as well? What about gathering information for the public, even if it is not legally required?

_____

_____

_____

_____

Do you agree or disagree with the legislature's push for greater openness? Why or why not?

_____

_____

_____

_____

How does your board handle requests to speak to the board during the citizen comment period? What about a request to appear on the agenda for a more detailed conversation with the board?

_____

_____

_____

_____

How does your board deal with persons it thinks are willfully interrupting, disturbing, or disrupting a meeting? Does it make use of G.S. 143-318.17, Disruptions of official meetings,[18] or does it folllow other procedures? What are they?

_____

_____

_____

_____

18. G.S. 143-318.17 is set out in Appendix 3.

Have you ever voted without fully understanding the issue before the board? What might you or the board do to ensure all members of the board understand the issues before them and are prepared to vote?

_____
_____
_____
_____

To what extent do you think transparency means information should be clear and understandable to the public?

_____
_____
_____
_____

Optional Section on Censure of Board Members

As noted earlier, the state law that requires local governing boards to adopt codes of ethics does not provide authority for enforcing them. In contrast, other state statutes and the common law do contain standards and, in some cases, specific remedies for violations of particular legal requirements. For the most part, the local board has no role to play in enforcing these laws, other than calling the violation to the attention of the district attorney or other proper enforcement authority.

A resolution censuring a member is the main action the board can take when it concludes that one of its members has violated its code. Such a resolution has no legal effect on the censured board member.

The board has no legal authority to create or impose other sanctions. For example, unless a board is covered by a specific local act of the legislature that provides otherwise (which is rarely the case), the board cannot legally require its members to sign pledges agreeing to obey the local code, or to produce financial disclosure statements, and it has no legal authority to punish members who refuse to do so. Indeed, since such requirements exceed a board's legal powers, it is probably unethical to try to establish them.

Below are suggested guidelines for a board to follow if it decides to include a censure procedure in its code. However, a strong caution is in order. Boards should consider carefully the implications for community and board trust and for an accused member's reputation before including such a procedure in the code or before beginning censure proceedings in particular cases. Censure is a serious measure, and it should not be entered upon lightly. The board's attorney should be involved at every step of the process, both to ensure that proper procedures are followed and to help the board members avoid making statements that might provoke accusations of libel or slander from the accused.

[Censure Procedures. If a majority of the board has reason to believe that one of its members has violated a provision of this Code of Ethics, it [shall] [may] open an investigation into the matter to determine whether probable cause exists to initiate censure procedings against the member. All information compiled, including the grounds for any finding of probable cause, shall be shared with the member when it is received. All information pertaining to the case shall be open to public inspection and copying pursuant to the North Carolina public records statutes. If upon investigation the board concludes that a violation of a criminal law may have occurred, it shall refer the matter to the local district attorney.

Should the board determine that it wishes to proceed further with censure proceedings, it shall call for a hearing, to be held at a regular meeting or at a special meeting convened for that purpose. Notice of the hearing stating its time, place, and purpose shall be given once a week for two successive calendar weeks in a newspaper having general circulation in the jurisdiction. The notice shall be published the first time not less than 10 days nor more than 25 days before the date fixed for the hearing. In computing such period, the day of publication is not to be included but the day of the hearing shall be included. Alternatively, the hearing shall be advertised on the jurisdiction's website for the same period of time, up to and including the date of the hearing. The notice shall state that a detailed list of the allegations against the member is available for public inspection and copying in the office of the clerk or secretary to the board.

The hearing shall be convened at the time and place specified. The hearing and any deliberations shall be conducted in open session in accordance with the North Carolina open meetings statutes.

The accused board member shall have the right to have counsel present, to present and cross-examine expert and other witnesses, and to offer evidence, including evidence of the bias of any other board member or the presiding officer. An audio or video and audio tape of the proceedings shall be prepared. Any and all votes during the hearing shall be taken by the ayes and noes and recorded in the board's minutes.

Once the hearing is concluded, it shall be closed by vote of the board. The presiding officer shall next entertain a motion to adopt a nonbinding resolution censuring the member based on specified violations of the code of ethics. Any motion made must be an affirmative one in favor of adopting a nonbinding resolution of censure. If the motion or resolution does not state particular grounds for censure under the code of ethics, the presiding officer shall rule it out of order.

If a motion to adopt a nonbinding resolution of censure stating particular grounds under the code of ethics has been made, the board shall debate the motion. The accused member shall be allowed to participate in the debate [but shall not] [and shall also be allowed to] vote on the motion to adopt the resolution.[19]

At the conclusion of the debate, the board shall vote on the resolution. If the motion to adopt the nonbinding resolution of censure is approved by a [majority] [two-thirds] [three-fourths] vote of those present and voting, a quorum being present, the motion passes and the nonbinding resolution of censure is adopted.[20]

The text of the nonbinding resolution of censure shall be made a part of the minutes of the board. Any recording of the board's proceedings shall be approved by the board as a permanent part of the minutes. The proceedings shall then be considered concluded, the board having done all it legally can with respect to the matter in question.]

[**Comment.** As noted earlier, North Carolina law provides very few remedies for local governing boards that believe one of their members has violated a local code of ethics. In a very few cities, recall elections are possible, and in extreme cases an old common law remedy called amotion *might* be available as a means for removing a board member from office.[21] G.S. 14-230, which deals with neglect of duty in office, provides for removal from office under very extreme circumstances. However, the local district attorney must choose to pursue a prosecution under the statute, which almost never occurs.[22]

19. Under both the city and the county voting statutes, persons may be excused from voting on matters involving their own financial interest or official conduct. See G.S. 160A-75 and G.S. 153A-44, respectively. A censure proceeding is a matter involving a member's official conduct, and the member accused in the proceeding should not take part in any votes that take place. Sanitary district boards and boards of education do not have such specific statutes about voting, and they may choose if they wish to have a different rule.

20. There is no legal authority for a board to create a supermajority voting requirement in cases such as this where such a requirement is not specified by statute. Instead, the default requirement of majority vote applies. The supermajority option is nevertheless included in the Model Code's text in recognition that, since the censure resolution is binding on no one, the number of votes required for adoption may be inconsequential. In addition, some local board attorneys may advise their boards to require a supermajority vote to help avoid possible misuse of the censure process for political purposes.

21. See Frayda S. Bluestein, "I Second that Amotion," *Coates' Canons,* UNC School of Government, October 28, 2009, http://sogweb.sog.unc.edu/blogs/localgovt/?p=1139, and David M. Lawrence, *Removing Local Elected Officials from Office in North Carolina,* 16 WAKE FOREST L. REV. 547–561 (1980).

22. There is also a chance that federal statutes relating to "honest services" and "misuse of office" may apply to local officials and their codes of ethics. See, e.g., 18 U.S.C. § 1341, 18 U.S.C. § 1343, and 18 U.S.C. § 1346. However, these laws are beyond the scope of this Code. Court cases currently pending may help to answer this question.

The reason for these limitations on local governing boards' powers is simple. Members of local boards such as city councils, boards of county commissioners, school boards, and sanitary district boards attain their seats and legal powers through actions of the state legislature and the voters. Legally, each of the members is an independent actor, subject only to minimal control by the others.[23] Unlike a self-governing private organization, which was created by persons who became its members and continues to exist under its members' control, the members of a local governing board have been given no general authority to discipline each other. Unless a specific statute allows more, the most a board can do is register its displeasure with a member's conduct, either by some form of political persuasion or by adoption of a nonbinding resolution censuring the member. Such a resolution is an effective way to make public the board's conclusion that a violation of the code has occurred and to provide information to the voters, who ultimately have the authority to take action against the board member in the next election.

This section sets out a rather detailed censuring procedure. The main reason for its level of specificity is to ensure fairness to the board member and to the member's reputation. It is perhaps more detailed than some boards would like, and they might adjust it accordingly, as long as fairness to the accused is maintained. Making the procedure somewhat complicated also serves to screen out mean-spirited accusations of ethics violations that are actually based on personal, political, or policy disputes. Most board members truly endeavor to be ethical. They may occasionally be misunderstood, however, or may have an honest policy or other dispute with their colleagues. Likely most citizens and board members do not want to waste time on mean, unfair, or irresponsible accusations.

The Model Code provides different options for how to proceed after the initial accusation has been made. Note that all parts of the proceedings, including the collection of relevant materials, the hearing, and the board's deliberations, are public, in keeping with the requirements of the open meetings and public records laws. For example, the open meetings law specifically forbids discussing the performance of members of the local governing board in closed session. See G.S. 143-318.11(a)(6).[24]

23. Of course, as we have discussed, an ethical public official may choose to place voluntary limits on that independence.

24. In contrast, the board is allowed to "plan, conduct, or hear reports concerning investigations of alleged criminal misconduct" in closed session. G.S. 143-318.11(a)(7). However, the board itself has no power to plan or conduct criminal investigations concerning one of its members, and it could only hear a report about a criminal investigation involving a board member if the district attorney or a law enforcement agency wanted to inform the board about the investigation.

Since there are no statutory guidelines for this type of hearing, the board is generally free to adopt its own rules, as long as those rules are fair and comply with existing law and generally accepted principles of parliamentary procedure. The board should also consider the extent to which whatever procedures it chooses comport with its code of ethics, which binds all of the board members.

A board has no legal authority to create a supermajority voting requirement in cases such as this in which the rule is not specified by statute. Instead, for adoption of a resolution of censure and for other votes during the proceeding, the default requirement of majority vote applies.

Nevertheless, the Model Code includes several voting options with respect to the adoption of the resolution (majority, two-thirds, three-quarters), in recognition that, as explained in note 20, the number of votes required for adoption may be inconsequential since the censure resolution is not legally binding. In addition, requiring a supermajority vote may help to prevent misuse of the censure process for political purposes.[25]]

Questions for Discussion

What do you think of censure as a remedy for code violations by board members?

_____
_____
_____
_____

Is there a downside to the censure process? What is it?

_____
_____
_____
_____

Can you think of other remedies that might be more effective? What are they?

_____
_____
_____
_____

25. See Note 20.

What other tools, if any, are at the board's disposal to enforce its code of ethics?

_____

_____

_____

_____

Appendix 1: Guidelines for Ethical Behavior

As noted at various points in the Model Code of Ethics, local governing boards have no legal power to bring criminal or other charges against their members or otherwise to directly control one another's behavior. At the same time, board members should be familiar with laws that may affect them in their actions as public officials,[1] and they should take care to avoid common pitfalls. For example, some boards have found it useful in avoiding legal conflicts of interest to start each meeting by asking members to voluntarily inform the board if any matter on the agenda might present a conflict of interest or might require the member to be excused from voting.

The following guidelines are designed to translate current legal requirements into specific behaviors board members should avoid.[2] While statutory provisions should be viewed as a minimum standard, board members should always consider whether there are ethical problems with other behaviors, even if such behavior does not violate criminal or other statutes dealing with conflicts of interest or other subjects.

1. **Avoid deriving a direct benefit from contracts in which you are involved in making or administering on behalf of the public agency.** (G.S. 14-234(a)(1); criminal penalty; note defined terms in the statute: *direct benefit, involved in making or administering a contract.*)

2. **Avoid attempting to influence others involved in making or administering a contract on behalf of the public agency, even if you aren't involved, if you will derive a direct benefit from the contract.** (G.S. 14-234 (a)(2); criminal penalty; note defined terms in the statute: *direct benefit, involved in making or administering a contract.*)

---

1. See, for example, many of the statutes referenced in the Comment to Section 1 of the Model Code and reproduced in Appendix 3.
2. Thanks to Frayda S. Bluestein of the UNC School of Government for authoring this part of the guidebook.

3. **Avoid soliciting or receiving any gift or reward in exchange for recommending, influencing, or attempting to influence the award of a contract by the public agency you serve.** (G.S. 14-234(a)(3); criminal penalty.)

4. **Consider the ethical and practical consequences of deriving a direct benefit from a contract authorized under any exception to the statute and weigh these considerations against the potential advantage to the public agency and to yourself. Follow reporting requirements to ensure transparency.** (G.S. 14-234(b); (d1).)

5. **Avoid participating in deliberations about or voting on a contract in which you have a direct benefit, when the contract is undertaken as allowed under any exception to the statute.** (G.S. 14-234(b1); criminal penalty.)

6. **Avoid using your knowledge of contemplated action by you or your unit, or information known to you in your official capacity and not made public, to acquire a financial interest in any property, transaction, or enterprise, or to gain a financial benefit that may be affected by the information or contemplated action. Avoid intentionally aiding another to do any of these things.** (G.S. 14-234.1; criminal penalty.)

7. **Avoid receiving any gift or favor from a current, past, or potential contractor.** (G.S. 133-32(a); criminal penalty.)

8. **Consider the ethical and practical consequences of accepting a gift or favor under any exception to the statutory prohibition, and follow reporting requirements to ensure transparency.** (G.S. 133-32(d).)

9. **Avoid voting on matters involving your own financial interest or official conduct.** (G.S. 160A-75; 153A-44.) **Identify and disclose these matters in advance so your board can determine whether you have a conflict allowing you to be excused by the board from voting. When in doubt, obtain an opinion from your local attorney about whether you must vote or may be excused.**

10. **Avoid voting on any zoning map or text amendment where the outcome of the vote is reasonably likely to have a direct, substantial, and readily identifiable financial impact on you.** (G.S. 153A-340(g); G.S. 160A-381(d).)

11. **Do not participate in or vote on any quasi-judicial matter, including matters that come before the board when the board is acting in a quasi-judicial capacity under G.S. 153A-345 or G.S. 160A-388, if participation would violate affected persons' constitutional right to an impartial decision-maker. Impermissible conflicts under this statutory standard include "having a fixed opinion prior to hearing the matter that is not susceptible to change"; "undisclosed ex parte**

communications [communications between a board member and someone involved in the matter that occur outside the official quasi-judicial proceeding]"; "a close familial, business, or other associational relationship with an affected person";[3] or "a financial interest in the outcome of the matter."
(G.S. 153A-345(e1), G.S. 160A-388(e1); violation of the constitutional standard by one member invalidates the entire vote.)

12. **Fulfill your statutory obligation to vote on all matters that come before you even when there are appearances of conflict, and only refrain from voting when there is a legal basis for being or a requirement to be excused from voting.**
(G.S. 153A-44; G.S. 160A-75.)

Questions for Discussion

Are the legal enforcement standards described above useful to you? Why or why not?

_____
_____
_____
_____

Which of the statutes set out in Appendix 3 would you like to have further explained (for example, G.S. 14-234.1, Misuse of confidential information, or G.S. 133-32, Gifts and favors regulated)? You may wish to make a note and ask your board attorney for additional information.

_____
_____
_____
_____

What else would you like to know about your ethical responsibilities as an elected official?

_____
_____
_____
_____

In what ways will your board's code of ethics be most helpful?

_____
_____
_____
_____

3. The terms in this phrase appear in G.S. 153A-345(e1) and G.S. 160A-388(e1), but they are not defined.

Appendix 2: Background Information on Codes of Ethics

This appendix to the Model Code of Ethics supplies additional information that may be useful to local board members as they develop their codes. It provides background reading on what codes of ethics typically cover, and it discusses the appropriate place of ethics codes in a broader program to promote an ethical climate in local government.

What Codes of Ethics Typically Cover

Three Approaches

Codes of ethics typically come in three basic types: aspirational, prohibitive, and a hybrid blend of the first two.[1]

Aspirational codes are those that are concerned primarily with how we ought to be. They state the norms of behavior toward which we aspire, through the use of both general provisions and more specific requirements. Aspirational codes typically emphasize widely accepted ethical principles. They speak, for example, of responsibility, integrity, fairness, avoidance of conflicts of interest, and the need to act diligently and responsibly and to inspire and maintain public confidence and trust.

Aspirational codes appeal to public officials' higher and better desires. They promote ethical behavior by challenging public officials to go beyond the letter of the law and to become the "especially responsible citizens" that a community needs to govern it.

Prohibitive codes, in contrast, recognize that public officials may sometimes act in a manner that is self-serving or otherwise incompatible with the public trust. They promote

---

1. This section and the rest of Appendix 2 are adapted from Chapter 3 of A. Fleming Bell, II, *Ethics, Conflicts and Offices: A Guide for Local Officials*, 2nd ed. (Chapel Hill: UNC School of Government, forthcoming spring 2010).

better behavior by prohibiting and specifying sanctions for conduct that is considered to be unethical.

Hybrid codes that combine aspirational features with prohibitions of certain acts also are common. They attempt to inspire good behavior while imposing penalties for behavior that falls below specified standards.

Which Approach Works Best?

Is it better to praise and inspire, or to warn and sanction, when one wants public officials to adhere to ethical principles? That is, should one use positive reinforcement to encourage ethical behavior or impose rules and laws that control behavior by threat?

At their best, the aspirational and prohibitive approaches should balance and reinforce each other and not give conflicting signals. Codes of ethics should appeal to humans' better nature, while at the same time keeping our darker side in check. This suggests that hybrid codes may be the most useful.

Michael Josephson, a leading researcher and speaker on ethical topics, defines several characteristics of an effective ethics code. According to Josephson,

1. The code *should be comprehensive, covering the full range of ethical principles that apply to public officials.*
2. It should contain a *statement of guiding principles* that sets the tone for the code and to which public officials may return as they construe the more detailed code provisions. In effect, this is the aspirational part of the code.
3. The code *should have prohibitive aspects* that specifically apply principles of behavior to situations that are reasonably likely to occur. At the same time, however, it should be realistic in the standard of behavior it expects.
4. Finally, the code *should be clear and unambiguous*, simple, and easy to read and use, with devices such as *indexes* to help make it accessible. It also *should include a commentary* with explanations and illustrations.[2]

Is it realistic to assume that a code embodying all of these characteristics can be drafted? Some qualities, such as comprehensiveness, simplicity, and ease of use, seem to point in contrary directions, even if they are not mutually exclusive.

The drafter of Josephson's ideal code will encounter an age-old problem in legal writing: how does one draft clearly and simply, with general enough language to cover a variety

---

2. Adapted from Michael Josephson, "Sample Codes and Policies," in *Ethics Corps: A Training Program on Teaching Ethics in the '90s*, materials from seminar held Nov. 29–Dec. 2, 1993, in Airlie, Va. (Marina del Rey, Calif.: Joseph and Edna Josephson Institute for the Advancement of Ethics, 1993), 3–5.

of situations, but, at the same time, draft specifically enough to avoid uncertainty and to make it reasonably possible to adhere to the code's commands? Furthermore, if the code of ethics is being drafted for local elected governing boards, the writer must also consider the limits imposed on such codes by various other laws and by a lack of specific statutory authorization to impose sanctions against local elected officials.

Creating an Ethical Climate: The Appropriate Use of Codes

Codes of ethics can help to provide certainty, accountability, and identity for public officials. While it can sometimes be challenging to draft and interpret codes, it is important to realize the advantages of using codes to create an atmosphere in which the public trust is upheld. At their best, codes can be powerful tools for improving the ethical climate of local government.

But there may also be some dangers to overcome in overemphasizing the code approach to ethical decision making. First, adopting a code of ethics may in some cases take away the incentive to think critically about one's behavior. Some public officials may show a tendency simply to obey the letter of the law (the code) without understanding or considering the underlying rationale for the code's provisions. At worst, one may become like the police officer who, when confronted with the fact that he had lied about a matter, responded that lying was not specifically prohibited by his department's code of ethics.[3]

Second, a code of ethics is only useful if those whom it affects are committed to what it says. The highest ranking officials in the organization must serve as role models in carefully following the code's provisions.

Third, a code that attempts to anticipate and deal with every sort of situation that a public official may confront will be so long and detailed that many public officials will be unable to understand or follow it.[4] And, as was just noted, a code that is not obeyed by the officials whom it covers will not be useful. Instead, cynicism will likely develop among citizens and among the public officials themselves. To put it in today's jargon, if one is going to "talk the talk," one also has to "walk the walk." Having no written code of ethics at all may be better for public confidence than having a code that is not understood or obeyed.

3. Incident reported by a participant in an ethics session of the Law Enforcement Executives Training Program, held on February 8, 1995, at the UNC School of Government.

4. North Carolina's ethics and lobbying laws for state officials may suffer from this flaw of too much complexity.

On the other hand, a code that is short enough to be workable will likely be quite general and provide few specific answers. It will probably require that officials weigh situations and make their own judgments.

Of course, engaging in a thoughtful discernment process can be a very good thing. If a workable code is one that encourages such deliberations, then local governing boards may want to help their elected and appointed officials learn how to think critically when ethical dilemmas arise.[5]

In short, while ethics codes are important, the development of skills in ethical decision making is perhaps even more important in maintaining the public's trust in its elected and appointed officials. The public trust can only be preserved if public officials take their calling seriously and make informed decisions that reflect the core ethical principles that they and their citizens share.

5. The ethics training courses offered by the UNC School of Government emphasize critical thinking about ethical and related legal dilemmas.

Appendix 3: Related Statutes

This appendix to the Model Code is intended for general reference. It contains the constitutional oath of office and the text of many of the North Carolina statutes related to ethical behavior, including those that are discussed in Appendix 1. It concludes with Session Law 2009-403, the local government ethics act.

North Carolina Constitution
Article VI
Suffrage and Eligibility to Office

Sec. 7. Oath.

Before entering upon the duties of an office, a person elected or appointed to the office shall take and subscribe the following oath:

"I, _____, do solemnly swear (or affirm) that I will support and maintain the Constitution and laws of the United States, and the Constitution and laws of North Carolina not inconsistent therewith, and that I will faithfully discharge the duties of my office as _____, so help me God."

North Carolina General Statutes

§ 14-230. Willfully failing to discharge duties.

If any clerk of any court of record, sheriff, magistrate, school board member, county commissioner, county surveyor, coroner, treasurer, or official of any of the State institutions, or of any county, city or town, shall willfully omit, neglect or refuse to discharge any of the duties of his office, for default whereof it is not elsewhere provided that he shall be indicted, he shall be guilty of a Class 1 misdemeanor. If it shall be proved that such officer, after his qualification, willfully and corruptly omitted, neglected or refused to discharge any of the duties of his office, or willfully and corruptly violated his oath of office according to the true intent and meaning thereof, such officer shall be guilty of misbehavior in office, and shall be punished by removal therefrom under the sentence of the court as a part of the punishment for the offense.

§ 14-234. Public officers or employees benefiting from public contracts; exceptions.

(a) (1) No public officer or employee who is involved in making or administering a contract on behalf of a public agency may derive a direct benefit from the contract except as provided in this section, or as otherwise allowed by law.

   (2) A public officer or employee who will derive a direct benefit from a contract with the public agency he or she serves, but who is not involved in making or administering the contract, shall not attempt to influence any other person who is involved in making or administering the contract.

   (3) No public officer or employee may solicit or receive any gift, reward, or promise of reward in exchange for recommending, influencing, or attempting to influence the award of a contract by the public agency he or she serves.

(a1) For purposes of this section:

   (1) As used in this section, the term "public officer" means an individual who is elected or appointed to serve or represent a public agency, other than an employee or independent contractor of a public agency.

   (2) A public officer or employee is involved in administering a contract if he or she oversees the performance of the contract or has authority to make decisions regarding the contract or to interpret the contract.

   (3) A public officer or employee is involved in making a contract if he or she participates in the development of specifications or terms or in the preparation or award of the contract. A public officer is also involved in making a contract if the board, commission, or other body of which he or she is a member takes action on the contract, whether or not the public officer actually participates in that action, unless the contract is approved under an exception to this section under which the public officer is allowed to benefit and is prohibited from voting.

   (4) A public officer or employee derives a direct benefit from a contract if the person or his or her spouse: (i) has more than a ten percent (10%) ownership or other interest in an entity that is a party to the contract; (ii) derives any income or commission directly from the contract; or (iii) acquires property under the contract.

   (5) A public officer or employee is not involved in making or administering a contract solely because of the performance of ministerial duties related to the contract.

(b) Subdivision (a)(1) of this section does not apply to any of the following:

   (1) Any contract between a public agency and a bank, banking institution, savings and loan association, or with a public utility regulated under the provisions of Chapter 62 of the General Statutes.

(2) An interest in property conveyed by an officer or employee of a public agency under a judgment, including a consent judgment, entered by a superior court judge in a condemnation proceeding initiated by the public agency.

(3) Any employment relationship between a public agency and the spouse of a public officer of the agency.

(4) Remuneration from a public agency for services, facilities, or supplies furnished directly to needy individuals by a public officer or employee of the agency under any program of direct public assistance being rendered under the laws of this State or the United States to needy persons administered in whole or in part by the agency if: (i) the programs of public assistance to needy persons are open to general participation on a nondiscriminatory basis to the practitioners of any given profession, professions or occupation; (ii) neither the agency nor any of its employees or agents, have control over who, among licensed or qualified providers, shall be selected by the beneficiaries of the assistance; (iii) the remuneration for the services, facilities or supplies are in the same amount as would be paid to any other provider; and (iv) although the public officer or employee may participate in making determinations of eligibility of needy persons to receive the assistance, he or she takes no part in approving his or her own bill or claim for remuneration.

(b1) No public officer who will derive a direct benefit from a contract entered into under subsection (b) of this section may deliberate or vote on the contract or attempt to influence any other person who is involved in making or administering the contract.

(c) through (d) Repealed by Session Laws 2001-409, s. 1, effective July 1, 2002.

(d1) Subdivision (a)(1) of this section does not apply to (i) any elected official or person appointed to fill an elective office of a village, town, or city having a population of no more than 15,000 according to the most recent official federal census, (ii) any elected official or person appointed to fill an elective office of a county within which there is located no village, town, or city with a population of more than 15,000 according to the most recent official federal census, (iii) any elected official or person appointed to fill an elective office on a city board of education in a city having a population of no more than 15,000 according to the most recent official federal census, (iv) any elected official or person appointed to fill an elective office as a member of a county board of education in a county within which there is located no village, town or city with a population of more than 15,000 according to the most recent official federal census, (v) any physician, pharmacist, dentist, optometrist, veterinarian, or nurse appointed to a county social services board, local health board, or area mental health, developmental disabilities, and substance abuse board serving one or more counties within which there is located no village, town, or city with a population of more than 15,000 according to the most recent official federal census, and (vi) any member of the board of directors of a public hospital if all of the following apply:

(1) The undertaking or contract or series of undertakings or contracts between the village, town, city, county, county social services board, county or city board of education, local health board or area mental health, developmental disabilities, and substance abuse board, or public hospital and one of its officials is approved by specific resolution of the governing body adopted in an open and public meeting, and recorded in its minutes and the amount does not exceed twenty thousand dollars ($20,000) for medically related services and forty thousand dollars ($40,000) for other goods or services within a 12-month period.

(2) The official entering into the contract with the unit or agency does not participate in any way or vote.

(3) The total annual amount of contracts with each official, shall be specifically noted in the audited annual financial statement of the village, town, city, or county.

(4) The governing board of any village, town, city, county, county social services board, county or city board of education, local health board, area mental health, developmental disabilities, and substance abuse board, or public hospital which contracts with any of the officials of their governmental unit shall post in a conspicuous place in its village, town, or city hall, or courthouse, as the case may be, a list of all such officials with whom such contracts have been made, briefly describing the subject matter of the undertakings or contracts and showing their total amounts; this list shall cover the preceding 12 months and shall be brought up-to-date at least quarterly.

(d2) Subsection (d1) of this section does not apply to contracts that are subject to Article 8 of Chapter 143 of the General Statutes, Public Building Contracts.

(d3) Subsection (a) of this section does not apply to an application for or the receipt of a grant under the Agriculture Cost Share Program for Nonpoint Source Pollution Control created pursuant to Part 9 of Article 21 of Chapter 143 of the General Statutes or the Community Conservation Assistance Program created pursuant to Part 11 of Article 21 of Chapter 143 of the General Statutes by a member of the Soil and Water Conservation Commission if the requirements of G.S. 139-4(e) are met, and does not apply to a district supervisor of a soil and water conservation district if the requirements of G.S. 139-8(b) are met.

(d4) Subsection (a) of this section does not apply to an application for, or the receipt of a grant or other financial assistance from, the Tobacco Trust Fund created under Article 75 of Chapter 143 of the General Statutes by a member of the Tobacco Trust Fund Commission or an entity in which a member of the Commission has an interest provided that the requirements of G.S. 143-717(h) are met.

(d5) This section does not apply to a public hospital subject to G.S. 131E-14.2 or a public hospital authority subject to G.S. 131E-21.

(d6) This section does not apply to employment contracts between the State Board of Education and its chief executive officer.

(e) Anyone violating this section shall be guilty of a Class 1 misdemeanor.

(f) A contract entered into in violation of this section is void. A contract that is void under this section may continue in effect until an alternative can be arranged when: (i) immediate termination would result in harm to the public health or welfare, and (ii) the continuation is approved as provided in this subsection. A public agency that is a party to the contract may request approval to continue contracts under this subsection as follows:

(1) Local governments, as defined in G.S. 159-7(15), public authorities, as defined in G.S. 159-7(10), local school administrative units, and community colleges may request approval from the chair of the Local Government Commission.

(2) All other public agencies may request approval from the State Director of the Budget.

Approval of continuation of contracts under this subsection shall be given for the minimum period necessary to protect the public health or welfare.

§ 14-234.1. Misuse of confidential information.

(a) It is unlawful for any officer or employee of the State or an officer or an employee of any of its political subdivisions, in contemplation of official action by himself or by a governmental unit with which he is associated, or in reliance on information which was made known to him in his official capacity and which has not been made public, to commit any of the following acts:

(1) Acquire a pecuniary interest in any property, transaction, or enterprise or gain any pecuniary benefit which may be affected by such information or official action; or

(2) Intentionally aid another to do any of the above acts.

(b) Violation of this section is a Class 1 misdemeanor.

§ 132-9. Access to records [from G.S. Chapter 132, Public Records]

(a) Any person who is denied access to public records for purposes of inspection and examination, or who is denied copies of public records, may apply to the appropriate division of the General Court of Justice for an order compelling disclosure or copying, and the court shall have jurisdiction to issue such orders. Actions brought pursuant to this section shall be set down for immediate hearing, and subsequent proceedings in such actions shall be accorded priority by the trial and appellate courts.

(b) In an action to compel disclosure of public records which have been withheld pursuant to the provisions of G.S. 132-6 concerning public records relating to the proposed expansion or location of particular businesses and industrial projects, the burden shall be on the custodian withholding the records to show that disclosure would frustrate the purpose of attracting that particular business or industrial project.

(c) In any action brought pursuant to this section in which a party successfully compels the disclosure of public records, the court shall allow the prevailing party to recover its reasonable attorneys' fees if attributed to those public records, unless the court finds the agency acted with substantial justification in denying access to the public records or the court finds circumstances that would make the award of attorneys' fees unjust.

Any attorneys' fees assessed against a public agency under this section shall be charged against the operating expenses of the agency; provided, however, that the court may order that all or any portion of any attorneys' fees so assessed be paid personally by any public employee or public official found by the court to have knowingly or intentionally committed, caused, permitted, suborned, or participated in a violation of this Article. No order against any public employee or public official shall issue in any case where the public employee or public official seeks the advice of an attorney and such advice is followed.

(d) If the court determines that an action brought pursuant to this section was filed in bad faith or was frivolous, the court shall assess a reasonable attorney's fee against the person or persons instituting the action and award it to the public agency as part of the costs.

§ 133-32. Gifts and favors regulated.
(a) It shall be unlawful for any contractor, subcontractor, or supplier who:
  (1) Has a contract with a governmental agency; or
  (2) Has performed under such a contract within the past year; or
  (3) Anticipates bidding on such a contract in the future
to make gifts or to give favors to any officer or employee of a governmental agency who is charged with the duty of:
  (1) Preparing plans, specifications, or estimates for public contract; or
  (2) Awarding or administering public contracts; or
  (3) Inspecting or supervising construction.
It shall also be unlawful for any officer or employee of a governmental agency who is charged with the duty of:
  (1) Preparing plans, specifications, or estimates for public contracts; or
  (2) Awarding or administering public contracts; or
  (3) Inspecting or supervising construction
willfully to receive or accept any such gift or favor.

(b) A violation of subsection (a) shall be a Class 1 misdemeanor.

(c) Gifts or favors made unlawful by this section shall not be allowed as a deduction for North Carolina tax purposes by any contractor, subcontractor or supplier or officers or employees thereof.

(d) This section is not intended to prevent a gift a public servant would be permitted to accept under G.S. 138A-32, or the gift and receipt of honorariums for participating in meetings, advertising items or souvenirs of nominal value, or meals furnished at banquets. This section is not intended to prevent any contractor, subcontractor, or supplier from making donations to professional organizations to defray meeting expenses where governmental employees are members of such professional organizations, nor is it intended to prevent governmental employees who are members of professional organizations from participation in all scheduled meeting functions available to all members of the professional organization attending the meeting. This section is also not intended to prohibit customary gifts or favors between employees or officers and their friends and relatives or the friends and relatives of their spouses, minor children, or members of their household where it is clear that it is that relationship rather than the business of the individual concerned which is the motivating factor for the gift or favor. However, all such gifts knowingly made or received are required to be reported by the donee to the agency head if the gifts are made by a contractor, subcontractor, or supplier doing business directly or indirectly with the governmental agency employing the recipient of such a gift.

§ 143-318.9. Public policy [from G.S. Chapter 143, Article 33C, Meetings of Public Bodies].

Whereas the public bodies that administer the legislative, policy-making, quasi-judicial, administrative, and advisory functions of North Carolina and its political subdivisions exist solely to conduct the people's business, it is the public policy of North Carolina that the hearings, deliberations, and actions of these bodies be conducted openly.

§ 143-318.16. Injunctive relief against violations of Article [33C, Meetings of Public Bodies].

(a) The General Court of Justice has jurisdiction to enter mandatory or prohibitory injunctions to enjoin (i) threatened violations of this Article, (ii) the recurrence of past violations of this Article, or (iii) continuing violations of this Article. Any person may bring an action in the appropriate division of the General Court of Justice seeking such an injunction; and the plaintiff need not allege or prove special damage different from that suffered by the public at large. It is not a defense to such an action that there is an adequate remedy at law.

(b) Any injunction entered pursuant to this section shall describe the acts enjoined with reference to the violations of this Article that have been proved in the action.

(c) Repealed by Session Laws 1985 (Reg. Sess., 1986), c. 932, s. 3, effective October 1, 1986.

§ 143-318.16A. Additional remedies for violations of Article [33C, Meetings of Public Bodies].

(a) Any person may institute a suit in the superior court requesting the entry of a judgment declaring that any action of a public body was taken, considered, discussed, or deliberated in violation of this Article. Upon such a finding, the court may declare any such action null and void. Any person may seek such a declaratory judgment, and the plaintiff need not allege or prove special damage different from that suffered by the public at large. The public body whose action the suit seeks to set aside shall be made a party. The court may order other persons be made parties if they have or claim any right, title, or interest that would be directly affected by a declaratory judgment voiding the action that the suit seeks to set aside.

(b) A suit seeking declaratory relief under this section must be commenced within 45 days following the initial disclosure of the action that the suit seeks to have declared null and void; provided, however, that any suit for declaratory judgment brought pursuant to this section that seeks to set aside a bond order or bond referendum shall be commenced within the limitation periods prescribed by G.S. 159-59 and G.S. 159-62. If the challenged action is recorded in the minutes of the public body, its initial disclosure shall be deemed to have occurred on the date the minutes are first available for public inspection. If the challenged action is not recorded in the minutes of the public body, the date of its initial disclosure shall be determined by the court based on a finding as to when the plaintiff knew or should have known that the challenged action had been taken.

(c) In making the determination whether to declare the challenged action null and void, the court shall consider the following and any other relevant factors:

(1) The extent to which the violation affected the substance of the challenged action;

(2) The extent to which the violation thwarted or impaired access to meetings or proceedings that the public had a right to attend;

(3) The extent to which the violation prevented or impaired public knowledge or understanding of the people's business;

(4) Whether the violation was an isolated occurrence, or was a part of a continuing pattern of violations of this Article by the public body;

(5) The extent to which persons relied upon the validity of the challenged action, and the effect on such persons of declaring the challenged action void;

(6) Whether the violation was committed in bad faith for the purpose of evading or subverting the public policy embodied in this Article.

(d) A declaratory judgment pursuant to this section may be entered as an alternative to, or in combination with, an injunction entered pursuant to G.S. 143-318.16.

(e) The validity of any enacted law or joint resolution or passed simple resolution of either house of the General Assembly is not affected by this Article.

§ 143-318.16B. Assessments and awards of attorneys' fees [in actions brought under Article 33C, Meetings of Public Bodies].

When an action is brought pursuant to G.S. 143-318.16 or G.S. 143-318.16A, the court may make written findings specifying the prevailing party or parties, and may award the prevailing party or parties a reasonable attorney's fee, to be taxed against the losing party or parties as part of the costs. The court may order that all or any portion of any fee as assessed be paid personally by any individual member or members of the public body found by the court to have knowingly or intentionally committed the violation; provided, that no order against any individual member shall issue in any case where the public body or that individual member seeks the advice of an attorney, and such advice is followed.

§ 143-318.16C. Accelerated hearing; priority [for actions brought under Article 33C, Meetings of Public Bodies].

Actions brought pursuant to G.S. 143-318.16 or G.S. 143-318.16A shall be set down for immediate hearing, and subsequent proceedings in such actions shall be accorded priority by the trial and appellate courts.

§ 143-318.17. Disruptions of official meetings.

A person who willfully interrupts, disturbs, or disrupts an official meeting and who, upon being directed to leave the meeting by the presiding officer, willfully refuses to leave the meeting is guilty of a Class 2 misdemeanor.

§ 153A-44. Members excused from voting.

The board [of county commissioners] may excuse a member from voting, but only upon questions involving the member's own financial interest or official conduct or on matters on which the member is prohibited from voting under G.S. 14-234, 153A-340(g), or 153A-345(e1). For purposes of this section, the question of the compensation and allowances of members of the board does not involve a member's own financial interest or official conduct.

§ 153A-340. Grant of power [from G.S. Chapter 153A, Article 18, Planning and Regulation of Development].

(a) For the purpose of promoting health, safety, morals, or the general welfare, a county may adopt zoning and development regulation ordinances. These ordinances may be adopted as part of a unified development ordinance or as a separate ordinance. . . .

    * * *

(g) A member of the board of county commissioners shall not vote on any zoning map or text amendment where the outcome of the matter being considered is reasonably likely to have a direct, substantial, and readily identifiable financial impact on the member. Members of appointed boards providing advice to the board of county commissioners shall not vote on recommendations regarding any zoning map or text amendment where the outcome of the matter being considered is reasonably likely to have a direct, substantial, and readily identifiable financial impact on the member.

§ 153A-345. Board of adjustment.

    * * *

(e1) A member of the board or any other body exercising quasi-judicial functions pursuant to this Article [18 of Chapter 153A] shall not participate in or vote on any quasi-judicial matter in a manner that would violate affected persons' constitutional rights to an impartial decision maker. Impermissible conflicts include, but are not limited to, a member having a fixed opinion prior to hearing the matter that is not susceptible to change, undisclosed ex parte communications, a close familial, business, or other associational relationship with an affected person, or a financial interest in the outcome of the matter. If an objection is raised to a member's participation and that member does not recuse himself or herself, the remaining members shall by majority vote rule on the objection.

§ 160A-75. Voting.

No member [of a city council] shall be excused from voting except upon matters involving the consideration of the member's own financial interest or official conduct or on matters on which the member is prohibited from voting under G.S. 14-234, 160A-381(d), or 160A-388(e1). In all other cases, a failure to vote by a member who is physically present in the council chamber, or who has withdrawn without being excused by a majority vote of the remaining members present, shall be recorded as an affirmative vote. The question of the compensation and allowances of members of the council is not a matter involving a member's own financial interest or official conduct.

An affirmative vote equal to a majority of all the members of the council not excused from voting on the question in issue, including the mayor's vote in case of an equal division, shall be required to adopt an ordinance, take any action having the effect of an ordinance, authorize or commit the expenditure of public funds, or make, ratify, or authorize any contract on behalf of the city. In addition, no ordinance nor any action having the effect of any ordinance may be finally adopted on the date on which it is introduced except by an affirmative vote equal to or greater than two thirds of all the actual membership of the council, excluding vacant seats and not including the mayor unless the mayor has the right to vote on all questions before the council. For purposes of this section, an ordinance shall be deemed to have been introduced on the date the subject matter is first voted on by the council.

§ 160A-381. Grant of power [from G.S. Chapter 160A, Article 19, Planning and Regulation of Development].

(a) For the purpose of promoting health, safety, morals, or the general welfare of the community, any city may adopt zoning and development regulation ordinances. These ordinances may be adopted as part of a unified development ordinance or as a separate ordinance. . . .

    * * *

(d) A city council member shall not vote on any zoning map or text amendment where the outcome of the matter being considered is reasonably likely to have a direct, substantial, and readily identifiable financial impact on the member. Members of appointed boards providing advice to the city council shall not vote on recommendations regarding any zoning map or text amendment where the outcome of the matter being considered is reasonably likely to have a direct, substantial, and readily identifiable financial impact on the member.

§ 160A-388. Board of adjustment.

    * * *

(e1) A member of the board or any other body exercising quasi-judicial functions pursuant to this Article [19 of G.S. Chapter 160A] shall not participate in or vote on any quasi-judicial matter in a manner that would violate affected persons' constitutional rights to an impartial decision maker. Impermissible conflicts include, but are not limited to, a member having a fixed opinion prior to hearing the matter that is not susceptible to change, undisclosed ex parte communications, a close familial, business, or other associational relationship with an affected person, or a financial interest in the outcome of the matter. If an objection is raised to a member's participation and that member does not recuse himself or herself, the remaining members shall by majority vote rule on the objection.

GENERAL ASSEMBLY OF NORTH CAROLINA
SESSION 2009

SESSION LAW 2009-403
HOUSE BILL 1452

AN ACT TO REQUIRE ALL CITIES, COUNTIES, LOCAL BOARDS OF EDUCA-
TION, UNIFIED GOVERNMENTS, SANITARY DISTRICTS, AND CONSOLI-
DATED CITY-COUNTIES TO ADOPT A CODE OF ETHICS FOR THE GOVERNING
BOARD AND TO REQUIRE THE MEMBERS OF THOSE GOVERNING BOARDS
TO RECEIVE EDUCATION ON ETHICS LAWS APPLICABLE TO LOCAL GOVERN-
MENT OFFICIALS.

The General Assembly of North Carolina enacts:

SECTION 1. Article 5 of Chapter 160A of the General Statutes is amended by adding a
new Part to read:
"Part 3A. Ethics Codes and Education Programs.
"§ 160A-83. Local governing boards' code of ethics.
(a) Governing boards of cities, counties, local boards of education, unified governments,
sanitary districts, and consolidated city-counties shall adopt a resolution or policy containing a code of ethics to guide actions by the governing board members in the performance of the member's official duties as a member of that governing board.
(b) The resolution or policy required by subsection (a) of this section shall address at
least all of the following:
  (1) The need to obey all applicable laws regarding official actions taken as a board
      member.
  (2) The need to uphold the integrity and independence of the board member's
      office.
  (3) The need to avoid impropriety in the exercise of the board member's official
      duties.
  (4) The need to faithfully perform the duties of the office.
  (5) The need to conduct the affairs of the governing board in an open and public
      manner, including complying with all applicable laws governing open meetings
      and public records.

"§ 160A-84. Ethics education program required.

(a)   All members of governing boards of cities, counties, local boards of education, unified governments, sanitary districts, and consolidated city-counties shall receive a minimum of two clock hours of ethics education within 12 months after initial election or appointment to the office and again within 12 months after each subsequent election or appointment to the office.

(b)   The ethics education shall cover laws and principles that govern conflicts of interest and ethical standards of conduct at the local government level.

(c)   The ethics education may be provided by the North Carolina League of Municipalities, North Carolina Association of County Commissioners, North Carolina School Boards Association, the School of Government at the University of North Carolina at Chapel Hill, or other qualified sources at the choice of the governing board.

(d)   The clerk to the governing board shall maintain a record verifying receipt of the ethics education by each member of the governing board."

SECTION 2. G.S. 115C-47 is amended by adding a new subdivision to read:

"(57)   To adopt a code of ethics. – Local boards of education shall adopt a resolution or policy containing a code of ethics, as required by G.S. 160A-83."

SECTION 3. G.S. 115C-50 reads as rewritten:

"§ 115C-50. Training of board members.

(a) All members of local boards of ~~education~~ education, whether elected or appointed, shall receive a minimum of 12 clock hours of training annually. The 12 clock hours of training may include the ethics education required by G.S. 160A-84.

(b) The training shall include but not be limited to public school law, public school finance, and duties and responsibilities of local boards of education.

(c) The training may be provided by the North Carolina School Boards Association, the School of Government at the University of North Carolina at Chapel Hill, or other qualified sources at the choice of the local board of education."

SECTION 4. Article 4 of Chapter 153A of the General Statutes is amended by adding a new section to read:

"§ 153A-53. Ethics.

(a) The board of commissioners shall adopt a resolution or policy containing a code of ethics, as required by G.S. 160A-83.

(b) All members of the board of commissioners, whether elected or appointed, shall receive the ethics education required by G.S. 160A-84."

SECTION 5. Article 1A of Chapter 160B of the General Statutes is amended by adding a new section to read:

"**§ 160B-2.3. Ethics.**
(a) The governing board shall adopt a resolution or policy containing a code of ethics, as required by G.S. 160A-83.
(b) All members of the governing board, whether elected or appointed, shall receive the ethics education required by G.S. 160A-84."

SECTION 6. Part 2 of Article 2 of Chapter 130A of the General Statutes is amended by adding a new section to read:

"**§ 130A-49.5. Ethics.**
(a) The governing board shall adopt a resolution or policy containing a code of ethics, as required by G.S. 160A-83.
(b) All members of the governing board, whether elected or appointed, shall receive the ethics education required by G.S. 160A-84."

SECTION 7. The resolution or policy containing a code of ethics that is required by G.S. 160A-83 shall be adopted by each municipality, county, local board of education, unified government, sanitary district, and consolidated city-county on or before January 1, 2011. The governing board may look to model local government codes of ethics for guidance in developing the resolution or policy.

SECTION 8. Except as otherwise provided in this act, this act becomes effective January 1, 2010. All members of governing boards covered by this act shall receive their initial training to comply with G.S. 160A-84 within 12 months after that date.

In the General Assembly read three times and ratified this the 28th day of July, 2009.

s/ Walter H. Dalton
President of the Senate

s/ Joe Hackney
Speaker of the House of Representatives

s/ Beverly E. Perdue
Governor

Approved 2:00 p.m. this 5th day of August, 2009

Appendix 4: Additional Resources

A. Fleming Bell, II. *Ethics, Conflicts, and Offices: A Guide for Local Officials.* 2d ed. Chapel Hill, N.C.: UNC School of Government, forthcoming spring 2010.

Frayda S. Bluestein. *A Legal Guide to Purchasing and Contracting for North Carolina Local Governments.* Chapel Hill, N.C.: UNC School of Government, 2004 ed. with 2007 supp.

David M. Lawrence. *Open Meetings and Local Governments in North Carolina: Some Questions and Answers.* 7th ed. Chapel Hill, N.C.: UNC School of Government, 2008.

David M. Lawrence. *Public Records Law for North Carolina Local Governments.* 2d ed. Chapel Hill, N.C.: UNC School of Government, forthcoming 2010.

Ethics for Local Government Officials. Chapel Hill, N.C.: UNC School of Government. 2010. www.sog.unc.edu/programs/ethics/index.php.

9781560116509